# The Japanese Red Army

Aileen Gallagher

The Rosen Publishing Group, Inc.
New York

*For my mother, Margaret Y. Gallagher,*
*who read to me and took me to museums*

Published in 2003 by The Rosen Publishing Group, Inc.
29 East 21st Street, New York, NY 10010

**Library of Congress Cataloging-in-Publication Data**

Gallagher, Aileen.
The Japanese Red Army / Aileen Gallagher.— 1st ed.
   p. cm. — (Inside the world's most infamous terrorist organizations)
Summary: Discusses the origins, philosophy, and most notorious
attacks of the Nihon Sekigun terrorist group, including their present
activities, possible plans, and counter-terrorism efforts directed
against them.
Includes bibliographical references and index.
ISBN 0-8239-3823-9 (lib. bdg.)
1. Nihon Sekigun. 2. Terrorism—Japan. 3. Terrorists—Japan.
[1. Japanese Red Army. 2. Terrorism—Japan. 3. Terrorists.]
I. Title. II. Series.
HV6433.J32 N544 2003
952.04—dc21

                                                              2002010599

*Manufactured in the United States of America*

# Contents

# Introduction

The Japanese Red Army (JRA) was a terrorist group that kidnapped government officials, murdered innocent civilians, took hostages, and hijacked several airplanes. Either under its own flag or in conjunction with other terrorist organizations, the JRA sought to end modern imperialism (when one country takes control of a weaker country's land or strongly influences its economy and political system), first in Japan and then throughout the world. JRA members felt that imperialism made the rich richer and the poor poorer. The group adopted a communist philosophy that was devoted to social and economic equality for all people around the world. The group chose to use violence and terror, however, to achieve its goals.

Most terrorist groups have narrow objectives. The Irish Republican Army seeks a united, independent Ireland. The Palestine Liberation Organization uses terrorist tactics in its fight for an internationally recognized Palestinian state. Perhaps the JRA was too far reaching. It sought nothing less than worldwide revolution and global domination, a goal that even far better organized and more popular political action groups would be hard-pressed to achieve. Professing to seek the

Emperor Hirohito *(second from left)* inspects a millet field during a tour of an experimental farm in December 1935. Under Hirohito, Japan veered in a warlike direction. Though he had only limited control of his army, Hirohito did little to restrain its extremely violent invasions of Manchuria and other parts of China in the years before World War II. Lacking the courage to oppose his generals and admirals, Hirohito reluctantly agreed to wage war on the United States, dragging it into WWII by attacking Pearl Harbor. The war would cost more than three million Japanese lives. In part, it was the legacy of this period of bloodshed, dictatorship, militarism, and invasion that the Japanese Red Army was reacting against.

liberation of men and women everywhere, the JRA instead inflicted harm on people who were in no position to end international imperialism. In so doing, the JRA became as great an agent of injustice as the governments it sought to overthrow.

# The Birth of
# the JRA

The JRA burst onto the international scene in 1970 with its first major terrorist attack—the hijacking of a Japan Airlines jet. The group's roots extend all the way back to the 1940s, however, and the political and social upheaval Japan experienced immediately following World War II.

## A New Spirit

After Japan surrendered to the United States on August 14, 1945, General Douglas MacArthur was put in charge of the U.S. occupying forces. This meant that he was essentially in charge of all of Japan as well. MacArthur's dream was to plant the seeds of democracy in a country that had known only monarchy and dictatorship throughout its long history. He felt that the key to creating a democratic spirit among the people would be found in education. At MacArthur's urging, the Japanese government increased from six to nine the required number of years that Japanese children had to attend school. Most important, the country established a university system like that in the United States. Higher education was now open to a majority of Japanese, where once it had been available to only a wealthy and privileged few.

General Douglas MacArthur signs the Japanese surrender documents on September 2, 1945, aboard the USS *Missouri* in Tokyo Bay. After Emperor Hirohito accepted responsibility for the war and offered to abdicate (step down from) his throne, MacArthur insisted that he remain as emperor and be granted immunity from prosecution as a war criminal. MacArthur realized that Hirohito could be a valuable partner in his plan to rebuild Japan in America's image.

To the youth of Japan, these universities offered not only educational opportunities, but also a new sense of excitement. For many of these students, attending university would be their first time living on their own, away from their parents' homes and exposed to new ideas and different perspectives. MacArthur tried to foster this invigorating enthusiasm for a new kind of society. He encouraged the students to challenge old ways of thinking in the hope that a free exchange of ideas and lively debate would begin to create a democratic tradition in Japan. The students responded with greater energy than even MacArthur could have imagined or desired. Debate turned into protests as students challenged what they felt were conservative teaching staffs that still represented the ideals of Japanese imperialism.

The students also demanded some control over their own education. In January 1947, Tokyo University was the first school to grant students some autonomy (the freedom to make their own decisions on university matters), allowing them to form a self-governing association. The association was given control of the dormitories, dining halls, and student centers, leaving the actual classroom leadership in the hands of the faculty and administrators. Other schools followed suit. Soon students no longer chose whether or not to join these associations; they were automatically made members immediately after they enrolled at their university or college. As a result, the associations grew in number and influence.

## Power in Numbers

The Japanese Communist Party tried to gather all of these separate groups into a single national student association. It was most successful with the All-Japanese Federation of Student Self-Governing Associations, or Zengakuren. By the end of 1948, nearly 60 percent of Japan's student population belonged to Zengakuren.

Rioting Japanese students, protesting the signing of a mutual security treaty between Japan and the United States, use ropes to pull down the iron gates outside the official residence of Japanese prime minister Kishi in June 1960. They then poured into the residence's courtyard and attacked four police riot trucks parked there. The wave of riots that gripped Tokyo in the spring of 1960 made many in the U.S. government fearful that Japan was teetering on the edge of a communist revolution.

As years went on, Zengakuren and other student associations like it only grew in power. The influence of the Japanese Communist Party was growing, too, and political leaders in Japan and the United States were growing concerned. General MacArthur, still in Japan, tried to purge or imprison communists working as teachers or leaders of student groups. In response, the students threatened to strike and boycott exams for several months in 1950. Hundreds of students were arrested. Student activism grew more feverish in the early 1950s, which became known as the Molotov cocktail era (named after the homemade fuel bombs hurled by protestors).

Campus rallies ignited a fire of political protest that continued to blaze throughout the 1960s. Students protested everything from the quality of their education to Japanese foreign policy, from agricultural issues to national security concerns. Meanwhile, Zengakuren members fought among themselves, with politically moderate students struggling against communist members for control of the group.

## The Red Army Faction

From this turmoil—especially the splintering of the student associations into various rival groups—was born the Red Army Faction (in Japanese, Sekigun-ha; a military arm of the Japanese Communist League), which would evolve into the Japanese Red Army in 1970.

The Red Army Faction provided a home for all those students who felt social and political change was possible only through the use of force. It was not content to protest only the policies of universities or the Japanese government. Instead, the Red Army Faction wanted to spread its communist revolution throughout the world. Its leaders wanted to overthrow the national government, take power, and then help revolutionaries around the world do the same in their countries.

By the late 1960s, the Red Army Faction claimed 400 members scattered throughout the country. Many of them also belonged to

Japanese prime minister Eisaku Sato *(right)* with U.S. president Lyndon B. Johnson in January 1965. Though once selected as a possible kidnapping target by the Japanese Red Army, Sato was celebrated worldwide for his commitment to promoting peace. In 1974, he was awarded the Nobel Peace Prize, the first Asian ever to receive the honor. The Nobel Committee emphasized his efforts to turn Japan away from militant nationalism in the postwar years and toward greater global cooperation and a peaceful foreign policy.

other splinter groups at the same time. Only about 150 came to be core members, fully committed to armed revolt. This central group had several ideas about how to further world revolution, including kidnapping Japanese prime minister Eisaku Sato. An operation of

## The Red Army's Early Goals: People, Guns, Money

In its early days, the Red Army's goals were very specific: acquire guns, raise money, and kidnap prominent citizens. The group's plans were categorized by the letters P, B, and M. The letter P stood for people, and those plans involved kidnapping government officials in exchange for releasing prisoners. The letter B meant guns, possibly stemming from the Japanese word for weapons, *buki*. The Red Army wanted not only to rob the few gun shops in the country, but also to negotiate the illegal purchase of weapons from other countries and sympathetic organizations. The letter M stood for money, which was necessary to fund the group's activities. Red Army members got in the habit of robbing banks near public transportation stations so they could quickly hop on a bus and escape, vanishing among the general population.

this sort would require a lot of training and discipline, which the Red Army Faction did not yet possess.

In order to prepare for the kinds of terrorist activities they hoped would spark a revolution, the Red Army Faction held its first training session on November 3, 1969. The meeting was at an inn in Daibosatsu Pass, a mountainous area outside Tokyo. Since the army had yet to obtain guns (access to guns was strictly controlled in Japan), the training revolved around the making and detonating of pipe bombs (crude but deadly explosives). Yet, at this early stage, the Red Army Faction had not mastered secrecy; as word of the training session went out to members, the police heard about it, too. At a dawn raid on

November 4, fifty-three participants were arrested. Red Army members would never again be so open about their plans and repeat the mistakes made at Daibosatsu Pass.

## The Emergence of the JRA

The overall mission of the Red Army Faction was unclear at best. The ideological leaders were in prison and could do little to guide the group's thinking. But another man, Tsuneo Mori, would change that. For two years he had been a low-ranking soldier in the Red Army who simply followed orders. In college, Mori befriended Takamaro Tamiya, who would later be the mastermind behind the group's first major strike—the hijacking of a Japan Airlines passenger plane. Takamaro urged Mori to join him in a splinter group of the Red Army Faction that would soon come to be known as the Japanese Red Army (JRA). Mori rose in the ranks until he was one of the more senior members not in prison. It was Mori who took control of the group's limited communications network. He was a man of action who preferred giving orders to discussing goals and ideals.

With Mori planning bank robberies (at which the JRA was very successful, stealing over $10 million in 1971 alone), arranging weapons acquisition, and selecting targets, his friend Takamaro was left to work on a plan for the group's overall direction. His strategy would provide the world with a dramatic introduction to the JRA, which would now embrace international notoriety and increasingly dangerous and violent activity. The JRA committed its first act of terrorism on March 30, 1970. In its aftermath, a new and even more ruthless JRA leader would emerge.

# Getting the
# World's Attention

The person who would put the Japanese Red Army on international most-wanted lists was unusual, to say the least. In a country like postwar Japan, which was dominated by men, the JRA's most notorious leader was a woman. Her name was Fusako Shigenobu. It was she who built alliances between the JRA and various terrorist groups in the Middle East, expanding the Red Army's lethal reach. It was she who would become the most visible and recognizable member of the JRA. Of all the JRA members operating around the world, it was she who became the most feared.

## A Child of Poverty

Fusako Shigenobu was born on September 20, 1945. Despite owning a shop, her family struggled to make ends meet. Shigenobu hated the way people treated her simply because she was poor. At school, teachers and students alike would mock Shigenobu, who never had money for lunch. Communism, a political philosophy that promised to eliminate poverty and make everyone equal, was attractive to the young Shigenobu. Like so many other young people of her day, she became involved with a student organization in college and participated in the violent student demonstrations of 1968. Through such activity she eventually became involved with the JRA.

## CHAPTER 2

In a photo dated June 21, 1985, JRA leader Fusako Shigenobu *(right)* is seen seated with Kozo Okamoto, a fellow Red Army member and one of three participants in the JRA's deadly 1972 attack on Lod Airport in Tel Aviv, Israel. Initially treated as a secretary and errand girl by the JRA, Shigenobu would rise through the ranks and wrest control of the group away from its male leaders. In so doing, she would also broaden the scope of the JRA's activities, moving beyond Japan to inflict terror throughout Europe, the Middle East, and Asia.

As a twenty-four-year-old student, Shigenobu worked as a hostess in a bar. Her boss said she "never looked like an extremist." But when the manager suggested Shigenobu get married, she said she would never do so. "The revolution is my lover!" she vowed, according to William R. Farrell in his book, *Blood and Rage: The Story of the Japanese Red Army*. At first her love of the revolution seemed unrequited. Despite the JRA's supposed commitment to equality, she was given the usual lowly tasks reserved for the group's women, such as renting space for meetings. Though she was not directly involved in the Daibosatsu meeting, she was critical of its disorganization and carelessness. Convinced she could run a far more effective and efficient organization, Shigenobu would make a move for leadership, but not until after the JRA's dramatic debut on the world stage.

## The JRA's First Strike

On the morning of March 30, 1970, most passengers on the Japan Airlines plane the *Yodo*, bound for the southwest Japanese city of Fukuoka from Tokyo, were looking out the window at Mt. Fuji. They never noticed that in the back of the plane there were several young passengers dressed in business suits who were busy removing samurai swords from tubes meant to store fishing rods. Suddenly one passenger rose from his seat and yelled, "Raise your hands! We are going to North Korea!" according to Farrell's *Blood and Rage*. The men rose and moved toward the cockpit, waving their swords menacingly. Though threatening, the hijackers promised to let all the passengers escape unharmed as soon as the plane landed in North Korea.

The pilot, faced with the first hijacking in Japan Airlines history, reasoned with the terrorists, who were all members of the Japanese Red Army. The plane, he said, did not have enough fuel to get to North Korea. The terrorists reluctantly agreed to land and refuel in South Korea when they realized that crashing in the Sea of Japan was the only other option. By the time the

## Mixed Feelings

For the passengers of the hijacked Japan Airlines plane, the experience was terrifying, but not as uncomfortable as they might have imagined. An American passenger on board later joked that the hijackers should be offered jobs by Japan Airlines. "They'll make good stewards. They cleaned up ashtrays, picked up paper from the floor, and even brought me a magazine to read." The plane's captain had a different perspective: "They were lunatics! I wish I could have killed them." The captain spent most of the long ordeal with a sword at his back.

Source: William R. Farrell's *Blood and Rage*

plane began its approach, the airport was crowded with members of the military and police, government officials, and the press.

Negotiations to free the hostages began. Eventually, the terrorists reached an agreement. The passengers (who at this point had been on the plane for seventy-nine hours) were released in exchange for the Japanese vice minister of transportation, Shinjiro Yamamura. After refueling, the plane then took off for Communist North Korea, where the JRA members expected to receive a warm welcome, an offer of shelter, and a friendly base of operations from which to plan future attacks.

When the *Yodo* finally landed in North Korea, Yamamura and the crew were released, as promised. The nine members of the JRA on board remained in North Korea. For the next eighteen years, the Japanese police told its people that the hijackers lived as "guests" of that country. Yet the exiled JRA members did not begin to lead quiet, law-abiding lives in their new country. The successful hijacking meant that Takamaro Tamiya, a senior leader of the JRA, was out of Japan and free to plan new attacks throughout Europe, Asia, and the Middle East. Other JRA members who had been on board the plane would carry on terrorist activities for the next eighteen years.

## A Change in Leadership and Direction

Though the hijacking seemed to be a victory for the JRA (more as a demonstration that the group could pull off a major terrorist act than for anything concrete that was achieved by it), it also left a leadership vacuum at the top. Many of the JRA's top leaders were now living in North Korea. Shigenobu sensed her opportunity and began to make a play for leadership of the group. After the hijacking, and under Shigenobu's influence, the JRA's plans would only grow bigger and bigger.

Shigenobu's idea was for the JRA to join a revolutionary movement already in progress, since the revolution in Japan did not seem to be gathering any momentum. The Japanese people, conditioned by thousands of years of imperialism and the obedience it demanded, were not very attracted to communist revolution. They were still licking their wounds following World War II and trying to get their bearings within the new democracy. As a result, most Japanese had little interest in violent political change and further upheaval. Other groups throughout the world, however, were trying to overthrow governments they viewed as imperialist. If Shigenobu had her way, the JRA would join them. The new international focus

Members of a Jewish militia, the Irgun, march through the streets of Tel Aviv on the eve of the declaration of the state of Israel in 1948. Israeli statehood coupled with the unresolved status of Palestinians living on the same land would provoke an enduring anger and bitterness throughout the Arab world. The Japanese Red Army would harness this rage and try to use it to spark global revolution in its collaborative attacks with Palestinian radical militants.

would make the JRA better known and more dangerous than it could ever have been operating only in Japan.

Shigenobu viewed Palestine as the most promising location for the JRA to form alliances with local terrorist groups. Since the creation of Israel in 1948, Palestinians have been fighting to end

Palestinian guerrillas patrol the streets of Amman, Jordan, in September 1970. Following the Six-Day War in 1967, Israel gained the Golan Heights from Syria, the West Bank from Jordan, and the Gaza Strip from Egypt. These territories newly occupied by Israel contained large Palestinian populations. Many Palestinians became refugees, escaping the occupying forces and seeking new homes in the neighboring Arab nations. Placed in refugee camps by their Arab hosts, Palestinian bitterness and unrest only grew. The JRA recognized the power of this anger and passionate desire for political and social change and saw it as a useful tool in its own violent revolutionary campaign.

what they view as an unlawful occupation of their homeland. Shigenobu saw this conflict as a revolutionary struggle against an oppressive, imperialist government that was backed by the United States, the biggest imperialist of all.

# Getting the World's Attention

Before her plan could be put into place, however, Shigenobu had to convince the JRA leadership that joining forces with extremist Palestinian groups was a good idea. Since most of the JRA's organizational core had been on the hijacked Japan Airlines flight to North Korea, group leadership in Japan was weak. Following the hijacking, Tsuneo Mori had assumed leadership of the JRA almost by default, but slipped easily into the role when his former colleagues and superiors disappeared into the skies. Many members of the JRA questioned Mori's ability to lead, however, opening the door to Shigenobu's growing influence.

Mori strongly disagreed with Shigenobu's plan. Whereas she believed that the overthrow of imperialism must be a global fight, Mori was convinced that it could and should start in Japan. Mori was not interested in sharing leadership. He felt the group could operate most effectively by placing all control with one person: himself. He did most of the recruiting and gave all the orders, and he wanted to keep it that way.

At first Mori refused to grant Shigenobu permission to leave the country on the grounds that no other JRA member had ever tried to begin chapters outside of Japan. She, in turn, threatened to quit the group and go it alone. Mori gave in. Though he refused to meet with Shigenobu directly, a messenger on his behalf asked her to go to Palestine as a representative of the Japanese Red Army. At this point, Mori became leader of the JRA's domestic branch, while Shigenobu led the group's international arm. Eventually she would emerge as the JRA's sole leader.

# A Deadly
# Collaboration

Shigenobu's arrival in the Middle East was perfectly timed to coincide with a growing desire among Palestinians to seek outside support for their anti-Israeli activities. Though Palestinians had long been struggling against Israel, they did so with little success. A full-scale Palestinian-Israeli war broke out in June 1967, but even an army aided by other Arab states (including Egypt, Jordan, and Syria) could not defeat Israel, which was backed financially and militarily by the United States. At that time, Palestinian leaders determined that conventional warfare, with traditional troops and weapons, would not defeat Israel. Terrorism and guerrilla warfare were now thought to be the only hope Palestinians had to remove Israel from the land they considered their own. The people of Palestine began to look for inspiration and assistance from other groups around the world who had fought to overthrow governments.

After the failure of the 1967 war, the Palestinian army dissolved into several splinter groups. One of these, called the Popular Front for the Liberation of Palestine (PFLP) was especially attracted to previous communist revolutions. Early on, the group, based in Lebanon, sought to form ties with other organizations that shared its vision of an armed revolutionary struggle followed by communist rule. The JRA was a perfect kindred spirit and a willing partner.

Palestine Liberation Organization (PLO) leader Yasir Arafat speaks on October 28, 1969, at a press conference in Syria, following Palestinian guerrilla attacks in Lebanon. Arafat founded one of the first militant Palestinian political groups, Fatah, in the 1950s. The group's ultimate goal was the creation of a Palestinian state, and it conducted terrorist attacks against Israel in an attempt to achieve this goal. In 1968, Fatah joined the PLO, as did the Popular Front for the Liberation of Palestine (PFLP). The JRA would form an alliance with the PFLP, and together the groups would launch some of the most deadly and violent terrorist attacks of the era.

## A Brother in Terror

An early JRA-PFLP collaborator was Kozo Okamoto. Kozo was the younger brother of one of the hijackers on the Japan Airlines jet *Yodo*, Takeshi Okamoto, who was more involved in the JRA than Kozo. Still, the younger Okamoto performed simple tasks for the group. In September 1971, a JRA member called Kozo Okamoto and offered him the chance to train in Beirut, the capital of Lebanon. The member suggested that if he went, Kozo would be reunited with his brother Takeshi, the hijacker living in exile in North Korea.

It took several months for Kozo to get to Beirut. By the time he arrived in Lebanon, he had flown from Tokyo to Montreal, then to New York, to Paris, and finally to Beirut. At a hotel in Beirut, Kozo was visited by Takeshi Okudaira, Shigenobu's husband and fellow JRA member. (Shigenobu entered a marriage of convenience that allowed her to slip out of Japan with a new surname.) Okudaira took Kozo to a camp outside Beirut. There, he trained for nine weeks with members of the PFLP. He underwent physical training and learned how to handle weapons and explosives. In his last week of training, Kozo learned his mission: He would participate in an attack on Israel's Lod (now called Ben-Gurion) Airport in Tel Aviv. The mission would go down in history as the JRA's bloodiest act, one that would place it among the world's most feared terrorist organizations.

Shigenobu was one of the masterminds behind the attack on Lod Airport. Through her relationship with the PFLP, she convinced the group that the JRA was perfect for the assignment. The PFLP was somewhat wary of the JRA. After all, the Japanese group wanted world domination, while the Palestinians were interested only in defeating Israel. With Shigenobu's urgings, however, the PFLP was convinced that JRA members would die for the Palestinian cause, and therefore were worthy and valuable comrades-in-arms.

The last stop for the terrorists before the Tel Aviv airport was Rome. Kozo Okamoto and two other JRA members acted like tourists during their three days in the Italian capital, visiting popular attractions and taking photographs. The waiter at their

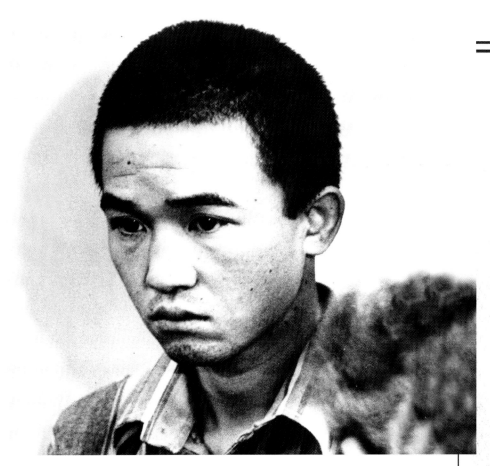

Kozo Okamoto during his military trial in Israel in July 1972. He was the only one of the three JRA members who took part in the attack on Tel Aviv's Lod Airport to survive. Though Okamoto expressed his desire to be executed or allowed to commit suicide, his defense lawyers entered a plea of temporary insanity. The judge sentenced him to life imprisonment. He would serve only thirteen years of that sentence. In 1985 he was released as part of a prisoner exchange between Israel and the PFLP and was sent to Libya. In the late 1990s, he would again be arrested in Lebanon for forging visas and passports and would serve three years in prison.

hotel remembered only that the three men had trouble eating spaghetti and did not tip him. On the morning they were to leave for Tel Aviv, Kozo went to his room and found a Czech automatic rifle, ninety rounds of ammunition, and hand grenades in his suitcase. The weapons had been personally delivered by Shigenobu.

## Attack in Tel Aviv

On May 30, 1972, 120 people flying from Puerto Rico landed in Tel Aviv. They were part of a religious group touring the Holy Land. The group went to the baggage claim area to collect their luggage. Three Asian men picked up bags and moved to a far wall, pretending to search through their suitcases. Suddenly, shots flew across the room. One eyewitness reported seeing twenty-five people piled up in a pool of blood. One attacker fired a submachine gun across the length of the room. Another threw grenades into several large groups of people. The third also threw grenades, first inside the terminal and then outside, hurling them toward planes.

The terrorists were not satisfied with simply attacking the baggage claim area. One began to fire through a glass partition into a waiting room beyond. Another fired his weapon through the baggage conveyor, aiming at airplanes on the runway. When his ammunition ran out, he tossed a grenade on the ground and threw himself on top of it in an apparent suicide (although some eyewitnesses said he threw the grenade, tripped, and fell on top of it). He was decapitated by the blast. A second attacker also lay dead, caught in the "friendly" crossfire of his comrades. That attacker was Takeshi Okudaira, Shigenobu's husband.

Though the attack lasted only a few minutes, it had devastating results. The wounded numbered eighty people, and twenty-four were dead. Of the dead, seventeen were part of the Puerto Rican pilgrimage group. Two of the terrorists were dead. The third—Kozo Okamoto—was arrested outside the airport. After running out of ammunition, he had dashed outside to throw a grenade at a

## A Father's Shame

Kozo Okamoto's father did not share his son's enthusiasm for the Israeli airport attacks. He was horrified that his two sons had turned to violence and killing. One, Takeshi, was a hijacker and the other, Kozo, a murderer. Mr. Okamoto sent a letter to the Israeli government following the Lod Airport attack that indicated his disgust with his sons' actions. "For forty years I thought I had devoted myself faithfully to the education of our young people. Please punish my son [Kozo] with the death sentence without delay," wrote Mr. Okamoto, as reported in the *Daily Yomiuri*.

plane. He surrendered immediately without resistance. In his mind, he had achieved greatness, according to Farrell's *Blood and Rage*. "When I was a child, I was told that when people died, they became stars. We three Red Army soldiers wanted to become Orion when we died. And it calms my heart to think that all the people we killed will also become stars in the same heavens. As the revolution goes on, how the stars will multiply!"

## A Death Wish Denied

A death sentence would have been welcomed by Kozo Okamoto—all he wanted was to die for the cause of world revolution. But it was not to be. Kozo would be denied again and again the one thing he wanted. To secure his confession, an Israeli military official promised him a gun and a bullet with which to commit suicide. Kozo never received the gun. At his

Blood and scattered luggage at Lod Airport (now called Ben-Gurion Airport) in Tel Aviv following the JRA attack on May 30, 1972. After receiving instruction in guerrilla tactics from Palestinian commanders in a PFLP training camp outside Beirut, Lebanon, three JRA members, including Takeshi Okudaira, husband of JRA leader Fusako Shigenobu, attacked the baggage claim area. Throwing grenades and opening fire with submachine guns, the three men killed twenty-four people and wounded eighty more.

trial, he repeatedly declined the opportunity to be represented by a defense attorney in hopes that he would be found guilty sooner and put to death. A military tribunal would not agree to try his case, however, until he had legal representation. Finally, when he was sentenced on July 18, 1972, the judge refused to grant Kozo his death wish. Instead, he was sentenced to spend the rest of his life in prison.

Kozo Okamoto was devastated by the sentence and continued to express his desire to be executed. In prison, Kozo experienced great psychological difficulty with solitary confinement. After being visited in prison by a Japanese religious group, he began to read the Old Testament. Soon he became convinced he was an agent of God and his acts at Lod Airport fulfilled God's plan. He was released from prison on May 20, 1985, as part of a prisoner exchange between Israel and the PFLP. He was sent to Libya, much to the dismay of the Japanese government, which protested his release. In Libya, Kozo received a hero's welcome. Shigenobu was there to greet him.

## The Aftermath of Lod

The sense of fear inspired by the attack at Lod spread across the globe. Months later it would be overshadowed when Palestinian terrorists kidnapped and murdered eleven Israeli athletes at the 1972 Olympics in Munich, Germany. People felt not only shock and horror at the idea of gunmen opening fire in the middle of an airport, but also a distinct fear. Since victims of such incidents are so often average, everyday people, there is a strong sense of "It could have been me." This is precisely the

## Strengthening a Bond

The Tel Aviv airport attack, which seemed so senseless to most of the world, was supported by many Palestinians. Two months prior, the Israeli army had killed two Palestinians who were trying to hijack a plane. Terrorism is often retaliatory in nature, an "eye for an eye" kind of violence. Thus, the attack at Lod Airport was justified by some as payback for the two prior Palestinian deaths. In fact, when news of the attack reached Palestinian refugee camps in Lebanon, crowds cheered in front of the house belonging to a widow of one of the dead hijackers. For months afterward, many newborn Palestinians were named after the three "martyred" members of the Japanese Red Army. Perhaps the biggest significance of the attack at Lod was how it solidified the relationship between the PFLP and the JRA. More important, other Arab extremist groups now viewed the JRA as sharing their cause. The Arab-JRA partnership would continue to grow.

reaction the JRA and the PFLP wanted to provoke. By unleashing terror in public places, terrorists make people afraid to follow their daily routines. When normal life is disrupted in this way, citizens may begin to exert pressure on their government to accommodate the terrorists' demands. In extreme cases, a government that cannot protect its citizens from terrorist attacks can become so unpopular that it may fall from power.

# Exchanging Hostages for Prisoners

The massacre at Lod Airport was a significant turning point for the Japanese Red Army. The group had started down a violent path, and it was not interested in turning back. In the year following the attack in Tel Aviv, the JRA continued to train new members and forge new alliances with other terrorist groups. Shigenobu had been successful in switching the JRA's attention to the Middle East. She remained in the Middle East, planning future attacks with the Popular Front for the Liberation of Palestine. Their next operation would be reminiscent of the first terrorist act to make the world take notice of the JRA: a hijacking. Unlike the first one, however, this hijacking would end in death and destruction. It would also mark the end of the JRA's collaboration with Palestinian extremists and the beginning of the group's slow unravelling.

## A Botched Hijacking

A JRA member named Osamu Maruoka was chosen to represent the group in its latest venture. On July 20, 1973, Maruoka boarded Japan Airlines Flight 404 from Amsterdam to Alaska. The 747 jet had six terrorists on board. Maruoka was the only JRA member aboard the plane; the other five were members of the PFLP. He posed as a new-lywed with a twenty-seven-year-old Christian Iraqi believed to be Katie George Thomas, who was the PFLP's chief operator in Europe.

# Exchanging Hostages for Prisoners

The pair sat in first class, drinking champagne, and then got up to go to the lounge for a cigarette (smoking was allowed on planes at the time). Thomas seemed to have trouble with her chair, and a flight attendant named Miyashita Yoshihisa went to help her. As Thomas bent over, a hand grenade fell out of her jacket and onto the floor. Before anyone could scoop it up, the grenade exploded. Thomas was killed instantly, and Yoshihisa was badly injured. "I heard a sound like thunder. I had never heard an explosion before . . . I raised my head and saw that the lady was sitting there dead," the flight attendant told the *Japan Times* on July 24, 1973.

After the explosion, the remaining terrorists leapt to their feet, armed with grenades and automatic pistols. They announced to the passengers and crew that they were taking over the plane. While they initially seemed to be in control and following a carefully laid-out plan, the entire operation quickly dissolved into chaos. Due to the JRA's insistence on secrecy and tightly controlled security, the only person who knew all the details of the hijacking—Katie George Thomas—was dead. This procedure was meant to prevent exposure of the plot if the authorities captured and interrogated any of the hijackers before the operation got underway. Terrorists cannot confess to what they do not know.

Without Thomas, the hijackers did not know what demands to make or where to take the plane. So they began to improvise. First, the hijackers demanded to land in Beirut. The airport there denied the landing request, however, saying that the runway was too short to accommodate a jumbo jet. The plane then circled aimlessly over the Mediterranean Sea until it was finally allowed to land in Dubai, in the United Arab Emirates. There, the jet idled on a desert runway for three days.

Japan Airlines Flight 404 burns on a runway at Benghazi Airport in Libya. The aircraft was hijacked by six terrorists, one from the JRA and five from the PFLP. Eighty-seven hours after the bungled hijacking began, the aircraft landed at Benghazi, the passengers and crew were released, and the plane was set on fire and ultimately destroyed. One of the terrorists, the only one who knew the entire plan and list of demands, was killed by her own grenade as the hijacking began.

Thomas's body and the wounded flight attendant were taken from the plane. An elderly couple was also released. Maruoka, assuming command of the hijacking, told passengers he had demanded $4 million from the Japanese government. Japan Airlines officials denied that any demands were ever made. The president of Japan Airlines told reporters that the whole situation was extremely frustrating because the terrorists never demanded anything, making a resolution impossible. The hijackers were ready to leave Dubai but had nowhere to go. Abu Dhabi in the United Arab Emirates and Saudi Arabia both declined to accept the plane. Finally, the Libyan government said the hijackers could land the jet there. Thomas's casket was loaded onto the plane and it took off for Benghazi Airport.

As soon as the doors opened upon landing, the passengers fled the plane. The pilot remained to make sure everyone had been evacuated. During his check, he noticed Thomas's casket lying in the middle of the first-class area with grenades piled on top of it. After his escape, the plane exploded. The terrorists were seen dancing around the flaming wreckage.

## Disorganization Reigns

The hijacking was an embarrassing disaster. It was poorly conceived, the performance was chaotic, the goals were unclear, and nothing was gained in the end. No other Palestinian groups supported this particular act. The largest of them, the Palestine Liberation Organization, went so far as to publicly criticize the hijacking. The Libyan government issued a statement saying it saw the hijacking as "a crime for which the perpetrators have not been able to give any justification" and vowed to prosecute the hijackers. The trial never took place, however, and the hijackers were released within a year. Their escape from justice would allow for more terrorist activity in the years ahead.

On January 31, 1974, two JRA members and two PFLP members tried to explode a Shell oil refinery on an island off Singapore. The group managed only to destroy one of the refinery's storage tanks, and the other fires were extinguished easily. Following this strike, no country agreed to take the attackers. So another group of PFLP terrorists attacked the Japanese Embassy in Kuwait, demanding the Singapore terrorists be given asylum (a safe haven free from prosecution) in that country. Kuwait at first refused to allow the terrorists into the country, but relented after strong urging from Japan.

## Changes in Location and Direction

With two bungled operations based in the Middle East, Shigenobu decided the time was right to seek other allies besides the PFLP. The Palestinians had only the goal of becoming an independent nation; the JRA still dreamed of global revolution. It seemed increasingly clear that their very different goals made joint operations difficult at best and ineffective at worst.

Shigenobu turned her attention to Europe. She felt that Paris would make a perfect base of operations. At the time, French police tended not to investigate terrorists very energetically as long as their acts occurred outside of France. More important to Shigenobu's emerging plan, there was already a significant Japanese population in France as well as several European divisions of Japanese companies. Shigenobu's idea was to kidnap Japanese businessmen and demand large ransoms from their employers that would help finance other JRA activities.

## An Imprisoned Leadership

Before "Operation Translation" (as the new plan was called) could even get underway, however, several important JRA operatives were arrested. Yutaka Furuya, one of the bombers of the Shell oil refinery, was detained at Orly Airport in Paris on July 28, 1974. A search of Furuya revealed that he was carrying three forged passports, counterfeit money, and a number of coded documents detailing the JRA's plans to attack Japanese embassies and companies in seven major European cities. The documents provided a sort of roadmap for police, helping them to find and arrest several JRA members already living in Paris.

Furuya was charged with only minor offenses relating to his fake passports and counterfeit bills. He was sentenced to less than a year in jail. Eight other JRA members were arrested and sent to Switzerland, which wanted nothing to do with them. So they were sent on to West Germany and then the Netherlands.

## Holding France Hostage

Similar to the assault on the Japanese Embassy in Kuwait following the Shell refinery bombing, some JRA members tried to mount a "rescue" operation of Furuya. In order to gain his release, the group would have to take hostages as bargaining tools. The target was the French Embassy in The Hague, the capital of the Netherlands. Joining the JRA for the operation was Carlos the Jackal, an independent terrorist who lent his services to extremist organizations all over the world. By the mid-1970s, he was wanted in twelve countries.

Yutaka Furuya, the JRA member whose release from prison was demanded by the three group members who stormed the French Embassy in The Hague, Netherlands, on September 12, 1974. The JRA took eleven hostages. On September 17, 1974, Furuya was released, and he and the hostage-takers were provided with a $30,000 ransom and a plane to take them to Syria where they were promised asylum.

# The Japanese Red Army

On September 12, 1974, armed with pistols and grenades obtained by Carlos the Jackal, three JRA members stormed the embassy. After capturing the ambassador's driver, they forced him at gunpoint to lead them to the ambassador's office. On their way there, they ran into a police patrol. Shots rang out, and one terrorist and two policemen were wounded. The terrorists pressed on, however, and seized eleven hostages, including the French ambassador, Jacques Senard.

For once, the JRA's demands were clear and simple: release Furuya by 3:00 the following morning or the hostages would be shot one by one. The JRA also demanded $1 million in ransom and a fully fueled and manned 707 jet. While negotiations were underway, Furuya was removed from prison under armed guard by members of France's Anti-Commando Brigade and taken to Schiphol Airport in Amsterdam to await the outcome. The Brigade was under orders from French prime minister Jacques Chirac to execute Furuya if any of the hostages were harmed.

While French officials continued to consider the demands, Carlos the Jackal decided to put more pressure on them. On a busy Sunday afternoon, he strolled into the Deux-Magots, a popular Parisian café, and dropped a grenade from a balcony overlooking a crowded sidewalk. While he escaped unnoticed and unharmed, the blast killed two and injured thirty-four. The Jackal threatened to bomb a movie theater next.

The following day, the French government released Furuya, gave the terrorists $300,000, and supplied them with an airplane. To this day, the French government insists that the café bombing did not at all influence its decision to meet the JRA's demands.

In a terrorist career that spanned three decades, Ilich Ramirez Sanchez, known as Carlos the Jackal, is accused of masterminding a series of deadly bombings, hijackings, and kidnappings across Europe, including the massacre of Israeli athletes at the 1972 Munich Olympics. In 1994, Carlos the Jackal was captured and charged with the murder of two French secret agents and a Lebanese fellow revolutionary. In December 1997, he was sentenced to life imprisonment. As he was led from the courtroom back to jail, he raised his fist and shouted in French, "Long live the Revolution!"

The Syrian government allowed the terrorists to land in Damascus, but only if they turned over the ransom money. To the Syrians, the ransom made the operation seem more like a crime than a political act. The terrorists agreed, much to Shigenobu's dismay. The whole purpose of setting up a European branch of the JRA was to make money to fund the group's activities, and Shigenobu had yet to meet that objective.

Adding to the JRA's woes, European police authorities were now on high alert for any signs of terrorist activity. All across the continent, suspected terrorists were being arrested and deported. Shigenobu knew the JRA would not survive in Europe under the pressure of this new police attention, but she vowed to free any members currently under arrest. In 1975, she kept her promise.

## Hostages for Prisoners: A Winning Formula

Five JRA terrorists invaded the offices of the American Consulate and the Swedish Embassy in Kuala Lampur, Malaysia, on August 4, 1975. There, they took fifty hostages. A note dropped from a window demanded the release of seven JRA members imprisoned in Japan, a helicopter to ferry the terrorists from the embassy to the airport, and a Japan Airlines plane to fly them to the destination of their choice. As reported by William Farrell, the note indicated the Japanese government had only four hours to respond to the JRA's demands: "The answer by Japanese authorities must only be yes. We will execute the hostages in case no answer is received or the answer is no." In addition to being an attempt to free jailed JRA members, the attack was also a response to Japanese, American, and Swedish imperialism, the note said.

Yutaka Furuya being set free in exchange for the eleven hostages held by the JRA in the French Embassy in The Hague, Netherlands. The JRA would have all its demands met by the French government, encouraging it to use hostage-taking as a means of gaining the freedom of its imprisoned members several more times in the coming years.

The Japanese government agreed to release all seven prisoners, but only five were willing to go. Of the two who refused release, one no longer agreed with how the JRA fought imperialism, and the other was ill and nearing his parole date. Back in the embassy, JRA members were shocked that two of their comrades refused to leave jail. So long as the Japanese government was making concessions, however, they were considering the mission a success. Libya agreed to allow the plane carrying the hostage-takers and released prisoners to land in its country, after making it clear that they were only doing so at the request of the Japanese government. No mention was made of the terrorists' future in Libya or of any possible prosecution. Upon landing, they remained free.

The Kuala Lampur operation was so successful that Shigenobu organized another one, this time in Dacca, Bangladesh. On September 28, 1977, JRA members hijacked a plane, once again hoping to secure the release of imprisoned comrades. The group also demanded a $6 million ransom for the safe return of the hostages. And once again, the Japanese government gave in to the demands. This time the hijackers and released prisoners flew to freedom in Algeria. It was a huge success for the JRA and a considerable embarrassment for Japan. The government now appeared weak and easily blackmailed and, like the passengers on a hijacked plane, a hostage to the JRA.

## Identity Crisis

Back in Libya, the remnants of the JRA began to dwindle and disappear from sight. At this time, the group numbered between only twenty-five and thirty-five serious members. The group reevaluated its goals and questioned its political identity. Was it still a group seeking world revolution, or had it gotten too close to the causes espoused by the Popular Front for the Liberation of Palestine? The identity crisis proved confusing to the point that the JRA published a report in 1981 saying that it was considering abandoning the use of violence in the pursuit of its goals.

## A September 11 Connection?

In the hours after the September 11, 2001, attacks on the World Trade Center in New York City and the Pentagon outside Washington, D.C., the Al Jazeerah satellite news channel received a call from someone who stated that the JRA claimed responsibility for the attacks. The caller said the attacks were in retaliation for the United States dropping atomic bombs on Hiroshima and Nagasaki in the last days of World War II. The claims of JRA responsibility were never verified, and most experts believe that Osama bin Laden's Al Qaeda terrorist network was behind the attacks.

Smoke billows from the towers of the World Trade Center in New York City after two hijacked jets crashed into them. The terrorist attacks of September 11, 2001, are generally attributed to Al Qaeda, a radical Islamic group led by Osama bin Laden, a wealthy Saudi expatriate.

In 1983, the JRA seemed to deepen its commitment to nonviolence when Shigenobu, in a rare interview with the Japanese press, said the group had "left the way of absolute terror." Their violent tactics, it seems, did little to attract new members over the years. But two months later, the JRA reversed itself again and tried to recruit new members interested in armed worldwide revolution. In a Japanese magazine sympathetic to the communist movement and quoted in Farrell's *Blood and Rage*, the group placed what was essentially a help-wanted ad: "We are based in the middle of nowhere, but if you come to join us, it won't be difficult to locate us."

# Conclusion

Despite its fresh attempts to recruit new members, the Japanese Red Army was never again as active or dangerous as it had been in the first half of the 1970s. Its leadership was too spread out to be effective. Some members were in prison in various countries and others were either hiding in Japan or in exile. Money was also a problem—the JRA had no funds with which to plan and launch an attack. Plus, it could find no other terrorist groups to join forces with to enhance its strength and resources. No other terrorist groups were as dedicated to overthrowing imperialism as the JRA. They were fighting that war on their own, and not doing a very good job of it.

The Red Army's activities in the 1980s were random and ineffective. In May 1986, the group fired mortar rounds at the embassies of Japan, the United States, and Canada in Jakarta, Indonesia. In June 1987, the JRA claimed responsibility for rocket attacks on the British and American Embassies in Rome. No one was hurt.

The majority of JRA leadership maintained a safe haven in North Korea (veterans of the 1970 hijacking of the Japan Airlines flight) and in Lebanon, where the JRA's main training camp was. Other leaders who had been imprisoned in Japan or Israel for terrorist activities were released to Libya when the JRA took hostages to secure their freedom (as happened following the Swedish Embassy attack). By the end of the twentieth century, the group was in the

JRA leader Fusako Shigenobu arrives in Tokyo following her arrest in Osaka, Japan, on November 8, 2000. Her arrest came after three decades on the run from the law. After emerging from the train that took her to Tokyo from Osaka, Shigenobu raised her handcuffed wrists high in the air, made a thumbs-up sign, and declared, "I am determined to fight on!"

press again as pressure mounted on the Japanese government to bring the terrorists to justice. In an editorial on March 20, 2000, the Japanese newspaper *Yomiuri Shimbun* urged the government to locate and arrest all members of the JRA who remained at large and destroy the remnants of their terrorist network.

The spate of arrests began in 1987, when Osamu Maruoka was arrested trying to enter Tokyo. The police were shocked to learn that the JRA member had been in and out of Japan several times since he left the country in 1971 for the Middle East. In response to his arrest, the JRA car-bombed a U.S.O. club (an American military recreational facility) in Naples, Italy, in 1988. Five people were killed. That would prove to be the JRA's final act, however, as international governments began to work together to finally put a stop to the group. JRA members were rounded up and detained in the Philippines, Romania, Peru, Nepal, Bolivia, and Jordan. All were deported back to Japan and placed under arrest.

The authorities had yet to locate and arrest Shigenobu, however, who many believed was still carrying on the JRA's mission in Libya and trying to establish bases in the Philippines and Singapore. Japanese officials never could have guessed that when they caught her it would be in Japan. She was arrested in Osaka on November 8, 2000. She had been hiding in Japan since July of that year. Shigenobu was fifty-five at the time of her arrest, but age did not seem to have mellowed her. With clenched fists, she proclaimed, "I am determined to fight on," according to Agence France Presse.

A few months in jail, however, seemed to change Shigenobu's mind. On April 14, 2001, shortly before the beginning of her trial for the 1974 attack on the French Embassy in The Hague, Shigenobu announced that she was dissolving the JRA. "I will disband the

## Where Are They Now?

**Yu Kikumura:** JRA operative. He was arrested in April 1988 while driving on the New Jersey Turnpike in a car loaded with explosives. He may have been planning an attack that would coincide with the JRA's bombing of a U.S.O. club in Naples, Italy, that killed five people, including a U.S. servicewoman. He was convicted and is serving a lengthy sentence.

**Yoshimi Tanaka:** One of the nine JRA members who hijacked a Japan Airlines plane to North Korea in 1970. He was arrested in 1996 on the Vietnamese-Cambodian border, suspected of being involved in a North Korean scheme to counterfeit U.S. dollars. He was eventually cleared of those charges but sent back to Japan to face charges on the hijacking incident. Tanaka publicly apologized and submitted a signed confession, admitting to the hijacking and assault charges. He was sentenced to twelve years in prison.

**Kozo Okamoto:** The only one of the three Lod Airport terrorists to survive the attack, which killed twenty-four people. He was released from Romia Prison in Lebanon in March 2000, where he had been imprisoned for three years for forging visas and passports. After his release he was granted asylum by Lebanon because he had waged war against the Israelis. Four other JRA members imprisoned on the same forgery charges were sent to Jordan, which turned them over to Japan. There, they were brought up on charges of attempted murder and forgery of official documents.

**Fusako Shigenobu:** Leader of the JRA. She was arrested by Japanese police in November 2000 after twenty-five years on the

JRA members Kozo Okamoto and Kazuo Tohira smile as a policeman removes their handcuffs in the courtroom during their trial on passport and visa forgery charges in Beirut, Lebanon, in June 1997.

run. She now faces conspiracy and attempted murder charges in connection with the 1974 attack on the French Embassy in The Hague, as well as charges related to passport violations. Following her arrest, police also seized two supporters who are accused of helping her avoid detection while in Japan.

At least six JRA leaders from the 1970s remain at large.

Japanese Red Army and launch new fights," she said in a statement to supporters, as quoted by the Associated Press. "Our struggle has been insufficient and wrong, as it failed to become part of the history rooted in Japanese society . . . I plan to begin new fights from Japan based on legal international solidarity that fits the era."

Other JRA members agreed with Shigenobu's new attitude. Wakabayashi Moriyake, a participant in the 1970 Japan Airlines hijacking who was offered safe haven in North Korea, said he had changed his mind about terrorism. "Our ideals and our political lines are different today," he told England's *Manchester Guardian* in 1988. "Terrorism is the method of those who have no confidence in the power of the people, and it cuts you off from the masses. We have been extremists, but are no longer so."

The United States seemed to take Shigenobu at her word, or at least took comfort that most JRA leaders were jailed. On October 5, 2001, the U.S. State Department removed the Japanese Red Army from its list of twenty-eight active foreign terrorist groups based on the fact that it had been inactive for several years, its membership had shrank, and much of its leadership was behind bars.

Given that Shigenobu—whose iron will and determination were probably single-handedly responsible for holding the dwindling remnants of the JRA together for almost thirty years—is now behind bars, it seems unlikely that the JRA will ever again appear on the State Department's list of foreign terrorist organizations. The group seems to have been undone by both a scope that was too large—world revolution and domination—and a lack of focus that included poor planning, sloppy operations, vague demands, and detours into Middle Eastern politics.

A van carries four JRA members to Tokyo District Court on March 20, 2000, where they would face murder and forgery charges. The day before, the suspects had been deported from Lebanon, which no longer offered them safe haven. They were then sent to Jordan, which also denied their asylum request, instead turning them over to the Japanese authorities.

It is ironic that a group that hoped to inspire the world's masses to overthrow their governments instead alienated them through their violent acts. Rather than inspiring a global people's revolution, the JRA instead created an international spirit of antiterrorist cooperation that would finally shut down its operations and imprison most of its leaders. Jailed and exiled JRA members were forced to confront the fact that the world they had hoped to set free wanted nothing more than to see them safely behind bars.

# Glossary

**alliance**  A close association of groups formed to advance a common interest or cause.

**asylum**  The offer of safe haven and freedom from prosecution.

**concession**  An admission or acknowledgment; to give up something during bargaining in order to gain something else.

**conventional warfare**  Fighting war with traditional weapons and forces, such as guns, bombs, and tanks.

**martyr**  Someone who suffers and dies for a cause.

**methodology**  An organized way of doing things; a systematized approach.

**notoriety**  The state of being known for some unfavorable act or quality.

**perpetrate**  To commit an act, usually a crime.

**reminiscent**  Reminding one of something similar that occurred in the past.

**rift**  A break in friendly relations.

**tribunal**  A committee or board appointed to judge a legal case.

# For More Information

Central Intelligence Agency (CIA)
Office of Public Affairs
Washington, DC 20505
(703) 482-0623
Web site: http://www.cia.gov

Centre for the Study of Terrorism and Political Violence
Department of International Relations
University of St. Andrews
St. Andrews, Fife KY16 9AL
United Kingdom
Web site: http://www.st-and.ac.uk/academic/intrel/
    research/cstpv

Federal Bureau of Investigation (FBI)
J. Edgar Hoover Building
935 Pennsylvania Avenue NW
Washington, DC 20535-0001
(202) 324-3000
Web site: http://www.fbi.gov

Federation of American Scientists (FAS)
Intelligence Resource Program
1717 K Street NW, Suite 209
Washington, DC 20036
(202) 454-4691
Web site: http://www.fas.org/irp/index.html

International Policy Institute for Counter-Terrorism
ICT at the Interdisciplinary Center Herzlia
P.O. Box 167
Herzlia 46150
Israel
Web site: http://www.ict.org.il

National Security Agency (NSA)
Public Affairs Office
9800 Savage Road
Fort George G. Meade, MD 20755-6779
(301) 688-6524
Web site: http://www.nsa.gov

National Security Institute (NSI)
116 Main Street, Suite 200
Medway, MA 02053
(508) 533-9099
Web site: http://nsi.org

# For More Information

Office of the Coordinator for Counterterrorism
U.S. Department of State
Office of Public Affairs, Room 2509
2201 C Street NW
Washington, DC 20520
Web site: http://www.state.gov/s/ct

Terrorist Group Profiles
Dudley Knox Library
Naval Post Graduate School
411 Dyer Road
Monterey, CA 93943
Web site: http://library.nps.navy.mil/home/

## Web Sites

Due to the changing nature of Internet links, the Rosen Publishing Group, Inc., has developed an online list of Web sites related to the subject of this book. This site is updated regularly. Please use this link to access the list:

http://www.rosenlinks.com/iwmito/jra/

# For Further Reading

Fridell, Ron. *Terrorism and Political Violence at Home and Abroad.* Berkeley Heights, NJ: Enslow Publishers, Inc., 2001.

Holliday, Laurel. *Why Do They Hate Me? Young Lives Caught in War and Conflict.* New York: Pocket Books, 2000.

Meltzer, Milton. *The Day the Sky Fell: A History of Terrorism.* New York: Random House, 2002.

Ousseimi, Maria. *Caught in the Crossfire: Growing Up in a War Zone.* New York: Walker & Company, 1995.

Sarat, Austin, ed. *Terrorism.* New York: Chelsea House, 1998.

Sonneborn, Liz. *Murder at the 1972 Olympics in Munich.* New York: The Rosen Publishing Group, Inc., 2002.

Stewart, Gail B. *Terrorism.* San Diego, CA: KidHaven Press, 2002.

# Bibliography

ArabicNews.Com. "Lebanon Releases a Member in the Japanese Red Army." March 22, 2000. Retrieved April 2002 (http://www.arabicnews.com/ansub/Daily/Day/000322/2000032259.html).

Asian Human Rights Commission. "Japanese Red Army Hijacker Jailed." February 15, 2002. Retrieved April 2002 (http://www.ahrchk.net/news/mainfile.php/ahrnews_200202/2421/).

BBC World Service. "Leader Disbands Japanese Red Army." April 14, 2001. Retrieved April 2002 (http://news.bbc.co.uk/hi/english/world/asia-pacific/newsid_1278000/1278023.stm).

Farrell, William R. *Blood and Rage: The Story of the Japanese Red Army*. Lexington, MA: Lexington Books, 1990.

Gero, David. *Flights of Terror: Aerial Hijack and Sabotage Since 1930*. Somerset, England: Haynes Publishing, 1997.

Hoffman, Bruce. *Inside Terrorism*. New York: Columbia University Press, 1999.

Japan Economic Foundation. "Legendary Japanese Red Army Leader Nabbed." January/February 2001. Retrieved April 2002 (http://www.jef.or.jp/en/jti/200101_020.html).

"Japanese Terrorist Group Disbanding." *London Free Press*, April 15, 2001, p. A12.

Manchester, William. *American Caesar: Douglas MacArthur, 1880–1964*. New York: Laurel Leaf, 1996.

Middle East News Online. "Japan's Red Army Claims Responsibility for U.S. Attacks: Al Jazeerah." September 11, 2001. Retrieved April 2002 (http://www.middleeastwire.com/newswire/stories/20010911_3_meno.shtml).

Pons, Phillipe. "A Farewell to Arms . . . But Not to Revolution." *Manchester Guardian Weekly*, September 25, 1988, p. 16.

Powell, Secretary Colin L. "Statement on Redesignation of Foreign Terrorist Organizations." U.S. Department of State. October 5, 2001. Retrieved April 2002 (http://www.state.gov/secretary/rm/2001/5255.htm).

U.S. Department of State. "Japanese Red Army." Terrorist Group Profiles. April 2001. Retrieved April 2002 (http://web.nps.navy.mil/~library/tgp/jra.htm).

Yuasa, Shino. "Red Army Still Strikes Terror Into Japan." Agence France Presse, March 18, 2000.

# Index

exiled members of, 17–18, 36,
    38, 47
and hijackings, 13, 16–18, 21,
    23, 32–37, 47, 50
leaders of, 13, 14–16, 18–21
origins of, 6–13
and the Popular Front for the
    Liberation of Palestine
    (PFLP), 22, 23, 24, 30, 31,
    32, 37, 44
renunciation of violence of, 44,
    46, 52
and September 11, 2001, 45
splintering of, 21
Jordan, 22, 49

**K**

Kikumura, Yu, 50
Kuwait, 37, 38

**L**

Lebanon, 22, 24, 31, 47
Libya, 30, 36, 44, 47, 49
Lod Airport, Israel, 24–27, 30, 31,
    32, 51

**M**

MacArthur, General Douglas,
    6–8, 9
Malaysia, 42–44
Maruoka, Osamu, 32, 36, 49
Middle East, 14, 18, 22, 32, 37,
    49, 52

Molotov cocktail era, 10
Mori, Tsuneo, 13, 20
Moriyake, Wakabayashi, 52

**N**

North Korea, 16, 18, 21, 47, 50, 52

**O**

Okamoto, Kozo, 23–25, 26–30, 51
    father of, 27
Okamoto, Takeshi, 23, 27
Okudaira, Takeshi, 24, 26
Olympic Games (1972 Munich), 30

**P**

Palestine, 4, 19–21, 22, 24
Palestine Liberation Organization
    (PLO), 4, 36
Pentagon, 45
Popular Front for the Liberation
    of Palestine (PFLP), 22, 23,
    24, 30, 31, 32, 37, 44

**R**

Red Army Faction, 10–13

**S**

Sato, Eisaku, 11
Saudi Arabia, 36
Senard, Jacques, 40
Shigenobu, Fusako, 14–16, 18–21,
    24, 25, 26, 30, 32, 37, 42, 44, 46

## About the Author

Aileen Gallagher is a private investigator of corporations and a freelance writer. Her work has appeared in the *National Law Journal* and the *New York Law Journal*, and on TheStreet.com and Ironminds.com. She has written two previous books for the Rosen Publishing Group, Inc.: *Walter Payton* and *Henry the Navigator*. She lives and works in New York City.

## Photo Credits

Cover, pp. 19, 20, 25, 28–29, 39 © Hulton/Archive/Getty Images; p. 1 © Pornchai Kittiwongsakul/Corbis; p. 5 © The Image Works; pp. 7, 23, 41 © AP/Wide World Photos; p. 9 © Bettmann/Corbis; p. 11 © Francis Miller/TimePix; pp. 15, 43 © Corbis; pp. 34–35 © Kyodo News Service; p. 45 © Peter Morgan/ TimePix; p. 48 © TimePix; p. 51 © Ahmed Azakir/AP/Wide World Photos; p. 53 © Kazuhiro Nogi/Corbis.

## Series Design and Layout

Nelson Sá